This doodle book belongs to:

_____

Your name

_____

Date

"Every great dream begins
with a dreamer.
Always remember, you have
within you the strength,
the patience, and the passion
to reach for the stars
to change the world."

—Harriet Tubman (1820-1913)

POCKET Doodles For Girls

ANITA WOOD
DRAWINGS BY JENNIFER KALIS

GIBBS SMITH
TO ENRICH AND INSPIRE HUMANKIND
Salt Lake City | Charleston | Santa Fe | Santa Barbara

First Edition
14 13 12 11 10   10 9 8 7 6 5

Text © 2010 Anita M. Wood
Illustrations © 2010 Jennifer Kalis

Published by
Gibbs Smith
P.O. Box 667
Layton, Utah 84041

1.800.835.4993 orders
www.gibbs-smith.com

Cover design by Black Eye Design
Manufactured in Manitoba, Canada in August 2010
by Friesens
Job #58227

Gibbs Smith books are printed on either recycled,
100% post-consumer waste, FSC-certified papers, or
on paper produced from a 100% certified sustainable
forest/controlled wood source.

ISBN 13: 978-1-4236-0755-7
ISBN 10: 1-4236-0755-4

This book is lovingly dedicated to the Saras in my life: my mom and my daughter.

My sincere thanks and appreciation to all my other girls, who advise, inspire, and encourage. Dreams do come true! You're holding one of mine.

—Anita Wood

For my mom, who does everything she can to support me.

—Jennifer Kalis

Send a text message to your BFF.

BFF! Draw her.

BFF 4EVR

I ♡ _____Cinderella_____.

Decorate your dream wedding cake.

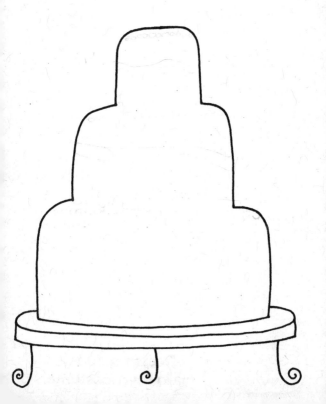

Design a funky
Halloween costume.

When I grow up, how many
kids do I want? Doodle
their names here.

Dear Diary—draw a cover
for your diary and design
a cute lock and key.

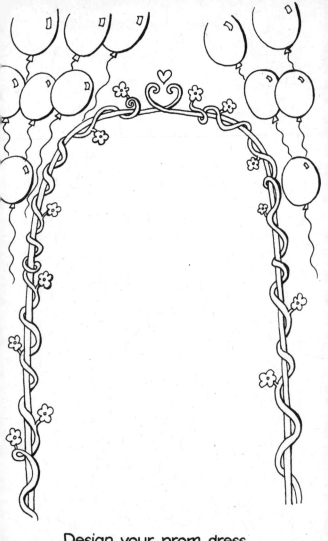

Design your prom dress.

Design the ultimate pair
of party shoes.

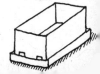

Carve a face on this pumpkin.

Put some toppings on this pizza.

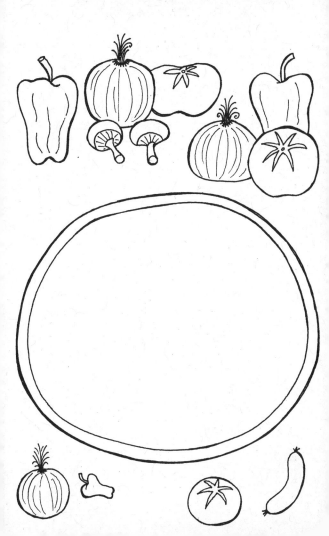

Two-piece or one? Design a knockout swimsuit.

First day of school outfit.
What will you wear?

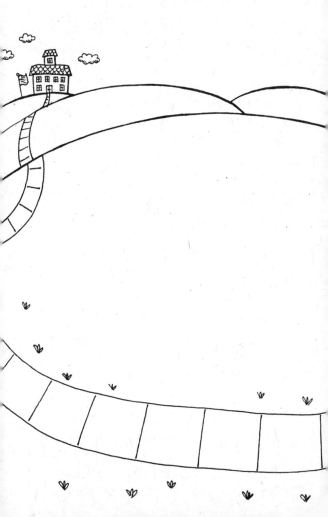

It's sunny outside. Design the coolest pair of shades ever!

Princess in the house! Design your signature tiara.

Birthday party swag bag! What would you send home with your friends? Design a cute bag to hold all the goodies!

Would you rather read minds or be invisible?

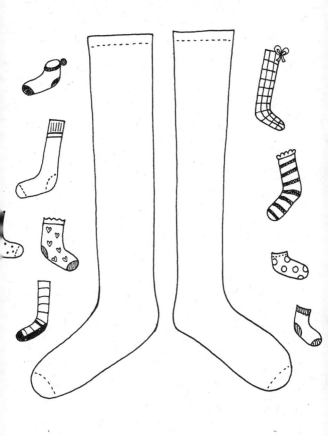

Draw a funky design
on these socks.

Flower power, baby!
Decorate this page with all
of your favorite blooms.

Who are your angels on earth?

SHH . . . secrets you just have
to tell or you'll absolutely bust!

_____

_____

_____

_____

_____

_____

_____

_____

_____

_____

_____

It's your turn to cook! Draw your favorite dinner.

Decorate these cookies.

My five fave actors are:

1.

2.

3.

4.

5.

Beauty Secrets! What do you
use to make yourself beautiful?

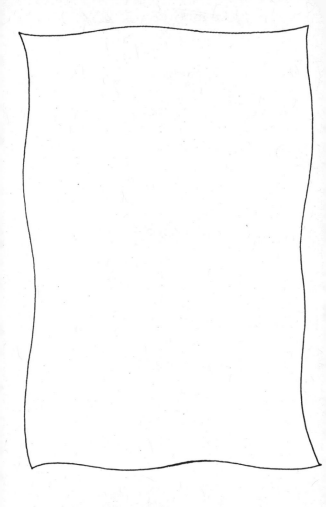

Stars, moons, flowers, or hearts?
Personalize your own stationery.

Hugs and Kisses XOX

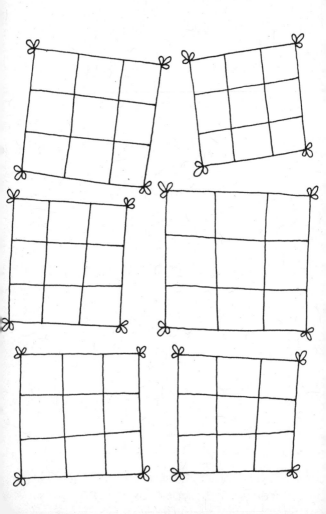

Glam up your pet!
Design an outfit for Fifi.

Write about a fairy tale with you in the role of the main character. What would you have done differently?

_____

_____

_____

_____

_____

_____

_____

_____

_____

_____

_____

_____

_____

_____

Things that totally ROCK!
Draw them here!

You're running for Class President. Write a catchy campaign slogan on this poster.

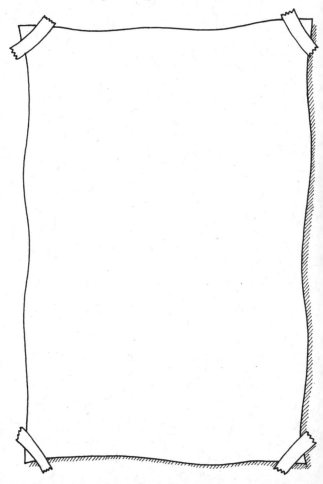

Fill this jar with your favorite candy.

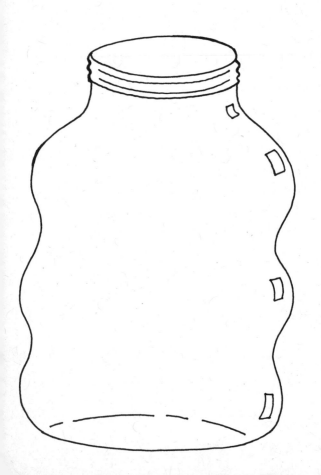

It's a "Bling Thing."
Design your own
signature piece
of jewelry.

If you could be a character in
a movie, who would you be?

Shop 'til you drop! You just won a shopping spree at your favorite store. What would you grab?

Glam up these high-top sneakers.

You just won the lottery! How are you going to spend all that money?

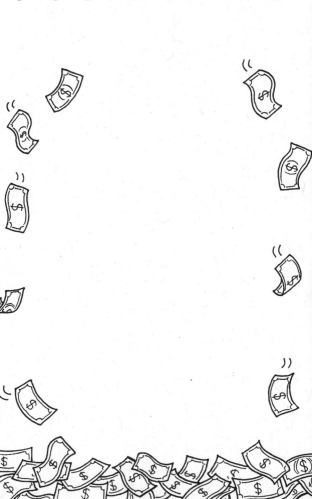

Who is your favorite
fairy-tale prince?

It's all about ME! Draw a self-portrait.

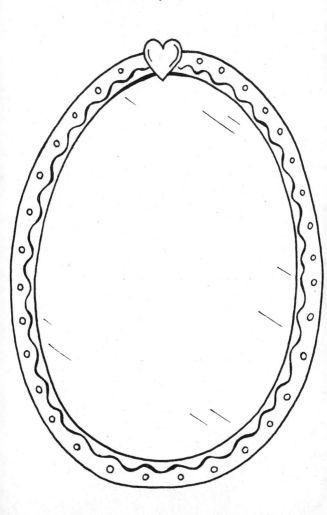

You just won a beauty contest!
Draw your fab evening gown.

You just found the cutest
pair of boots. Draw them.

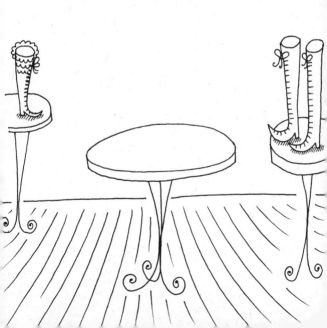

You made cheerleading
tryouts and won best uniform
design. Draw it here.

Denim Diva. Designer jeans by moi!
Put your fabulous design here.

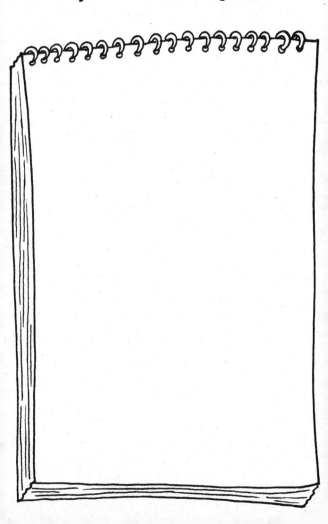

Best dream
I've ever
had is . . .

Plan a slumber party. What will you do? Games? Makeovers? Movies?

Rollerblades or ice skates?
Design the coolest pair EVER!

Decorate your dream bedroom.

If you were a car, what would you be?

Practice your signature for
when you're famous!

In the Pink! Draw a picture
of anything you want using
different shades of pink.

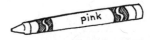

Draw your favorite
slippers and jammies.

TraumaRama! Most embarrassing moments . . .

Design your own trendy T-shirt.

Be prepared! I can't leave the
house without . . . what?
Draw it here.

What gives you goosebumps?
Draw it . . . if you dare!

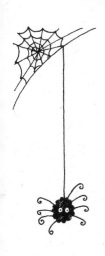

If you were a shoe, what
kind would you be?

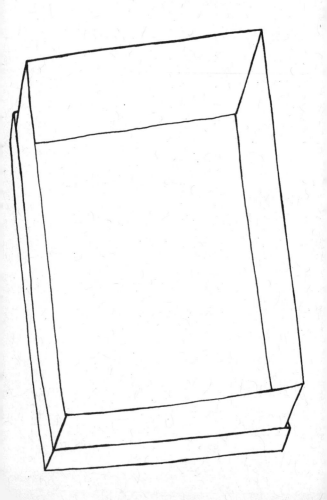

You're a world-famous chef
and your signature dish
is . . . Draw it here.

What grosses you out?

Write your name down the
side of this page and write one
positive word about yourself
that starts with each letter.

If you could go anyplace in the world, where would you go? Draw it.

What's happening right now?
This very minute! Write it!

_____

_____

_____

_____

_____

_____

_____

_____

_____

_____

_____

_____

_____

I want to grow up to be . . .

Draw the first thing that
comes to mind when you
see the following words:

Love

Cupcake

Homework

Summer

Best friend

Sports

My five favorite actresses are:

1.

2.

3.

4.

5.

If you could have any animal
in the world as a pet, what
would it be? Draw it here.

Design the cutest flip-flops ever!

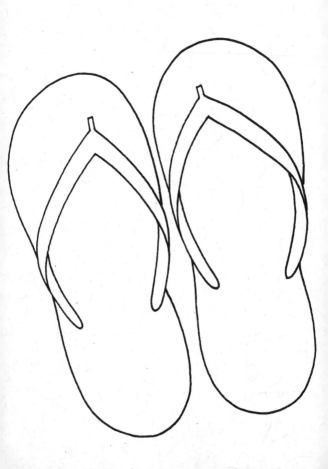

Who do you admire most?

What are the five most important things to you?

1

2

3

4

5

My favorite season is . . . Draw something that you like to do.

Hip pockets—draw a funky design for these jeans pockets.

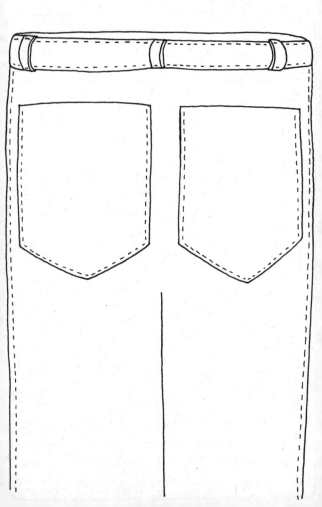

The Adventures of _____.
Draw a comic strip.

If you could meet anyone
living, who would it be?

Musical Notes: I wish I could
be in this band . . . Draw
yourself with them.

Is there a song playing in
your head right now?

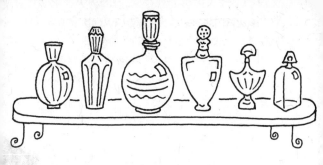

SCENTsational! Design a
perfume bottle and name
your special fragrance.

What a drag! I have to get up
at this time to get ready for
school. Give this clock some
hands and decorate its face.

Chill out! Build a snowchick.

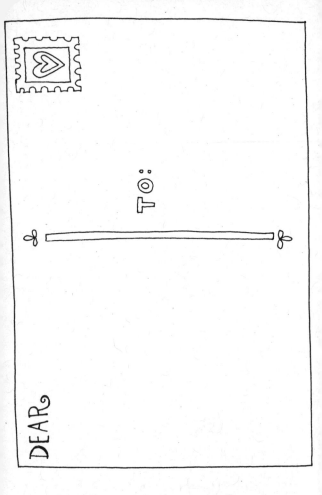

Greetings from . . . Write a
postcard to someone from a
place you would like to visit.

What's in your
backpack?

Personalize your license plate.

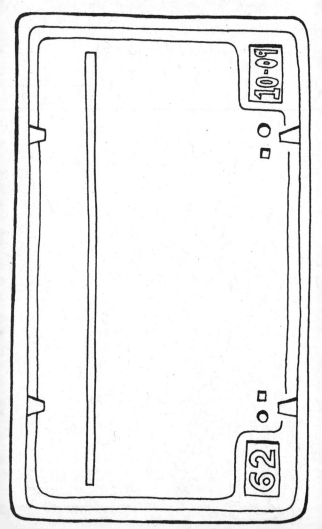

If you could meet anyone
from history, who would it be?
What would you talk about?

Start a gratitude journal! Write five things you are grateful for.

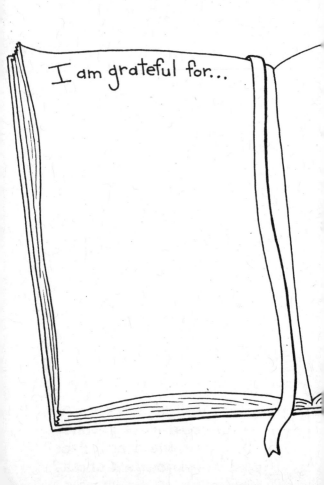

I am grateful for...

You discovered a new
species of butterfly!
Name it and draw
a picture of it.

Five things I like about ME!

1.

2.

3.

4.

5.

You just freed a genie from a magical lamp and have been granted three wishes. What will they be?

Zebras aren't the only cool things with stripes! Design a rockin' outfit here.

Stranger than fiction! You just wrote a best-selling book. What is it about? What is its title?

You just signed up as a volunteer. What do you do?

Volunteer

My favorite color is _____.

It smells like _____.

It tastes like _____.

It feels like _____.

Draw something that best
describes this color.

Discover your roots. Ask your grandma and grandpa to tell you something about their lives. Write it down here.

_____

_____

_____

_____

_____

World's youngest CEO! Design the logo for your company.

You've just been presented with a major award! What did you do to earn it? Draw it here.

What's your sign, baby?
Write your horoscope.

Your very own theme song
plays whenever you enter
a room. What is it?

My most favorite outfit—I could live in it 24/7. Draw it here.

You are a hip new fashion designer. Draw your signature piece of clothing.

Out of control! What's the craziest thing you ever did? Did you get caught?

You are the hottest new star in Hollywood. Are you keeping your real name or changing it? What would you change it to?

You just graduated from
high school. Now what?

How can you make a contribution to the world?

Draw a face to go with this nose.

If you were cereal, what
kind would you be?

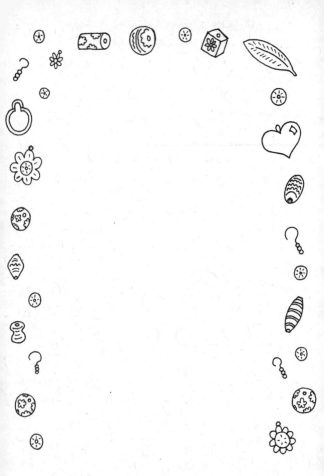

Design a funky pair of earrings.

What would you put into a time capsule?

You've invented the world's
BEST EVER chocolate bar.
Package it and name your treat.

Finding your bliss. What makes
you happy? Write or draw here.

You've been invited to a
masked ball. Decorate this
mask that you'll wear.

Sticky situation! Put some of your favorite stickers here.

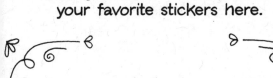

In the news: create today's headlines.

Press a flower or leaf here.

Draw a snowflake or a bunch of 'em!

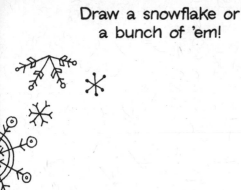

Are there words that make you giggle every time you hear or say them? How about

periwinkle

Hooligan

Serendipity

Shenanigans

to get you started!

You are what you eat! Collect the
little stickers off bananas, apples,
oranges, and so on. Put them here.

Do you believe in fairies?
Draw one.

Thanks, Mom! Write her a letter.

_____

_____

_____

_____

_____

_____

_____

_____

_____

_____

_____

Send yourself everywhere! Design
a postage stamp featuring YOU!

Girls Rule, Boys _Drool_.
Draw a sign to hang on
your bedroom door.

Collect your friends' fingerprints using different colors of ink. Make funny pictures out of them.

Design your own hot air balloon, and then take off to . . . where?

Save your movie and concert tix and attach them here.

A MIA
OCT 19 ☐

EAT 23A

CONCE
1 TICK
GREE
DAY

ENT
1
UG 23, 2009

Using small dots only, draw
a picture of whatever
strikes your fancy.

Write your favorite quote, poem, or saying here.

Draw your family as stick figures. Don't forget your pets!

ME

Write a bedtime story for the kids you babysit.

_____

_____

_____

_____

_____

_____

_____

Things that make me totally cranky. Doodle or write about them here.

Some things I'd like to do before I'm

You just ran away with the circus! Would you rather be a trapeze artist or a clown? Draw your fabulous costume here.

Would you rather be an astronaut or an archeologist? Describe and draw your discovery.

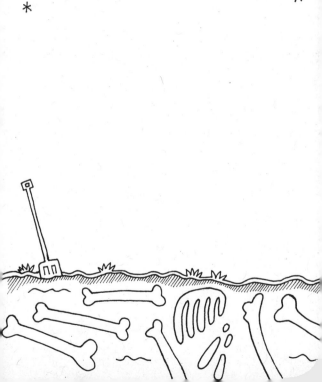

Fill these empty fortune cookies with good fortunes.

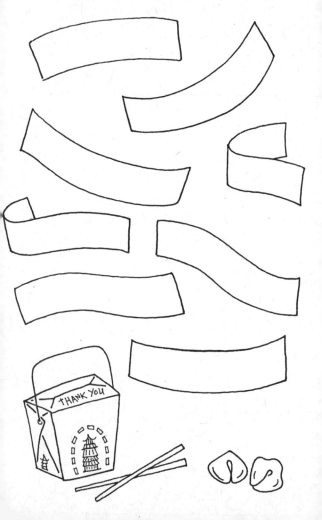

Smileys everywhere. Draw as many different ones as you can.

Pig out! Draw your favorite junk food.

Lucky me! What's your lucky
number? Lucky charm?

Dot to dot . . . Play the game here!

You see your future in a reflecting pool. Draw what you see.

5 reasons my BFF rocks!

1.

2.

3.

4.

5.

Trace your hand and adorn
it with some jewels!

Stone age chick!
You've just discovered
an ancient cave with
markings on the wall.
Draw what you see.

Queen of everything! Design your own royal emblem.

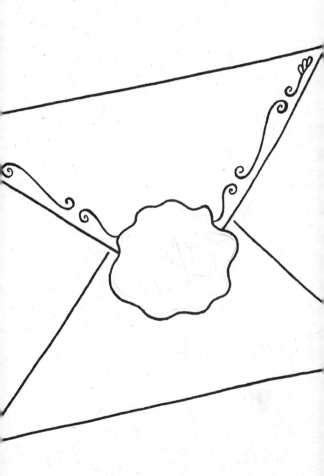

If you could control your life with a remote, where would you go?
Fast-forward to?
Rewind to?
Pause?

Sweet grooves. Design the tread on these shoes!

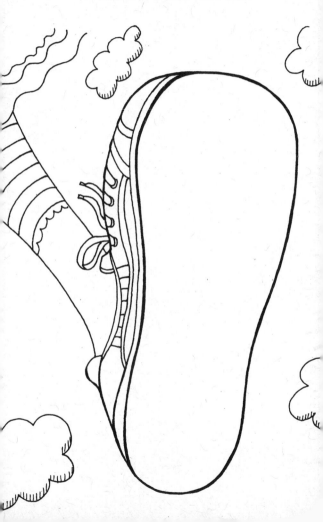

Let's go fly a kite! Design your own right here.

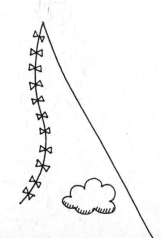

What are the most outrageous
chocolate-covered things you
can think of? Draw them here.

Rewrite one of your favorite nursery rhymes to include you.

_____

_____

_____

_____

_____

_____

_____

_____

_____

_____

Gourmet ice cream by
you! Create your own
signature flavors and scoop
them onto this cone.

Fill this old jar with some cute fireflies.

Design a matching piece of jewelry for you and your BFF.

Bad hair day? Create an instant
solution by designing a new:
Scarf   Headband
Hat   Scrunchie

Define your style: Hippie
or Preppy? Wild Child or
Girlie Glam? Draw it.

Ten things I love about . . . who?

1.

2.

3.

4.

5.

6.

7.

8.

9.

10.

Design your dream car.

Girls in Charge! What changes would you make if you were President?

Are you superstitious? About what? Draw or describe it.

Have you ever
had a great idea
for something that
would make your life
easier? Draw your
invention here.

It's been a zoo lately! What kind of animals do the following people remind you of? Mom, Dad, Siblings, Best Friend, Boyfriend.

Spring has sprung! What's growing in your garden? Draw it.

If you could talk to your
pet or a favorite animal,
what would you say?

Custom design a faceplate
for your cell phone.

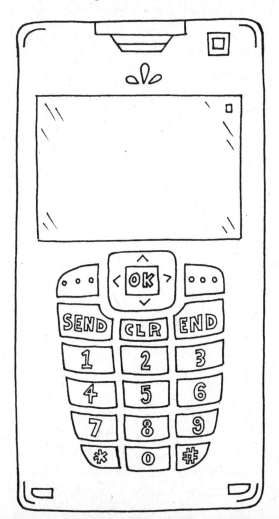

Bedtime secrets . . . do you
still have a favorite blanky or
stuffed animal you just can't
fall asleep without? Does it
have a name? Draw it here.

Describe these in one word:

School

_____

Music

_____

Family

_____

Friends

_____

Design your dream wedding announcement.

Do you play a musical instrument?
What kind? If not, what would
you like to learn? Sketch it here.

We are family! Who's on your family tree?

Undersea adventure. You're a
mermaid! Draw your treasures here.

Venus de Milo needs a makeover!
Give her an updated look.

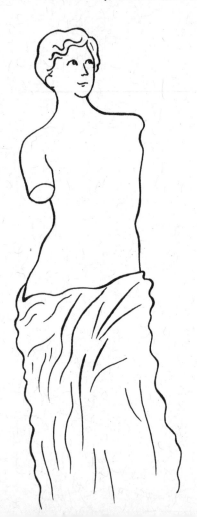

Draw your own artistic masterpiece.

Create the ultimate ice cream banana split sundae.

What would you eat for dinner every day if you could? Draw it here.

Where is heaven on earth
for you? Draw it.

Write a message on this mirror with lipstick. Be sure to blot it.

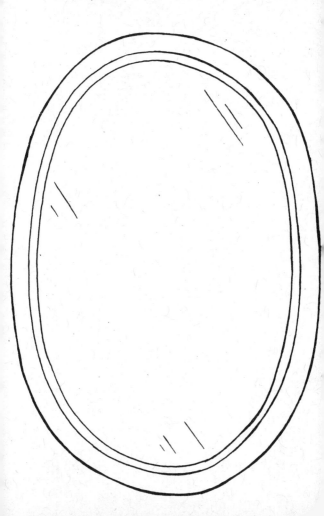

Five girls who really rock and why.

1.

2.

3.

4.

5.

Plaid is Rad! Draw a funky plaid design on these!

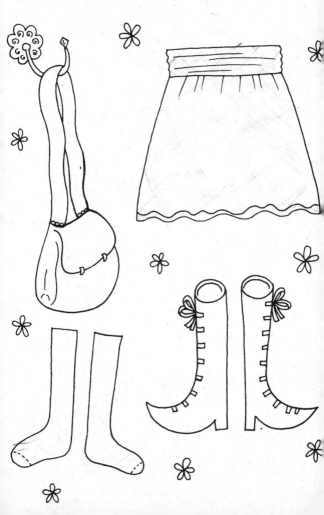

Funky fringe! Add some fringe here.

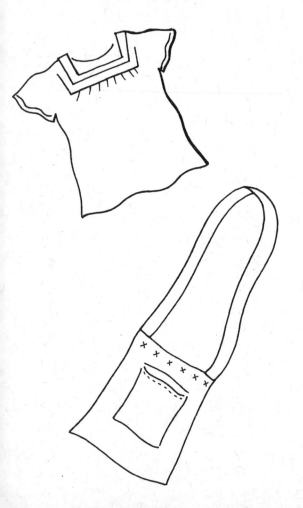

What do you see? A face
or a tree? Draw it.

Fill the Easter basket.

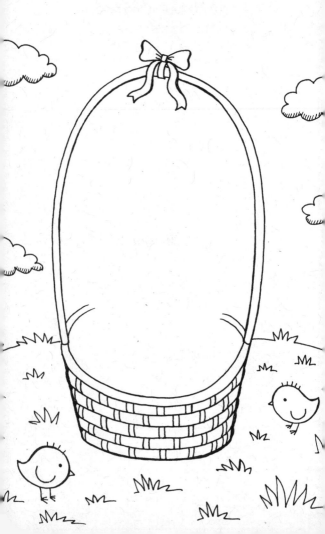

Your bowl of alphabet soup
just sent you a message.
What does it say?

The best burger ever would look like this . . .

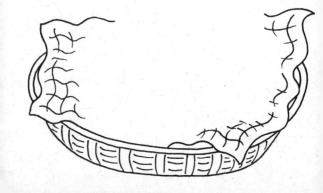

Would you rather skydive or hang glide? Custom design your glider or parachute here.

Write a scary story to tell around the fire during your next campout.

_____

_____

_____

_____

_____

_____

_____

_____

No Boys Allowed! Draw some plans for the ultimate treehouse here.

You are a detective.
What did you find?

Draw yourself as a paper doll and give yourself some stylin' clothes.

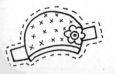

Smell-O-Rama! What would your sneakers say to you if they could talk?

Incredible shrinking girl! You've been shrunk to the size of a mouse and now live in a shoe box with a matchbox for a bed. Furnish your new room with things you've found lying around the house.

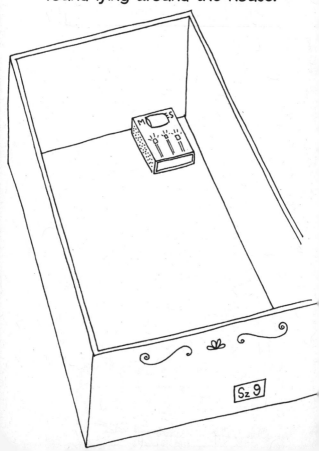

Secret agent! Follow somebody around for a day and take notes on what she does without her knowing.

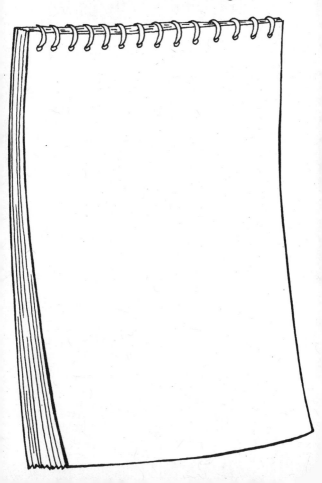

Jean-ious! How many holes are in your favorite pair of jeans? Draw them.

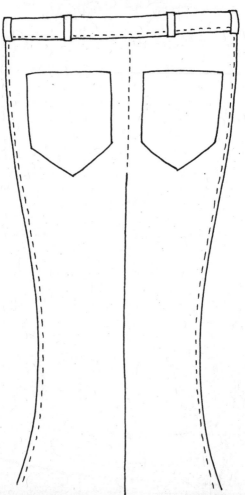

The "flea" circus is in town.
Draw the famous fleas here.

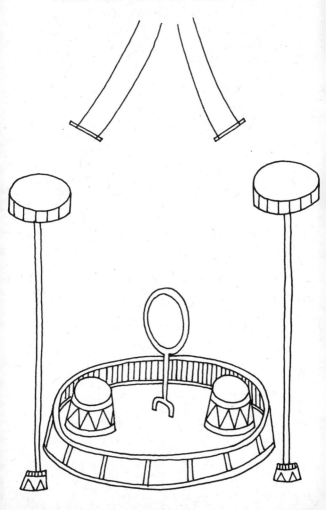

Design a CD cover for your fave band or singer.

Your bedroom closet opens a door to a secret world. What is it like? Draw it here.

You've discovered the "Lost City
of Gold" and brought home a
few souvenirs. What did you
grab? Draw them here.